Poiema

Poiema

Poems by D. S. Martin

D. S. MARTIN

WIPF & STOCK · Eugene, Oregon

POIEMA
Poems by D. S. Martin

Copyright © 2008 D. S. Martin. All rights reserved. Except for brief quotations in critical publications or reviews, no part of this book may be reproduced in any manner without prior written permission from the publisher. Write: Permissions, Wipf and Stock Publishers, 199 W. 8th Ave., Suite 3, Eugene, OR 97401.

Wipf & Stock
A Division of Wipf and Stock Publishers
199 W. 8th Ave., Suite 3
Eugene, OR 97401

www.wipfandstock.com

isbn 13: 978-1-55635-856-2

In memory of
Margaret Avison
(1918–2007)

"For we are his workmanship..."
— Ephesians 2:10

"To be human is to be completely alien amid the galaxies."
— Czeslaw Milosz

Contents

Acknowledgments xi

PART ONE WORLDS DESCEND FROM WORLDS 1

    Cædmon
    Behind My Eyes
    These Things Never Change
    Living in the Shadow
    Censorship
    The First Five Days—Amiens
    Tribal Burial Customs
    Ode to an Antique Sideboard
    Adrift
    The Pump at the End of the Lane
    Mongrel Mind

PART TWO THE KNIFE STILL FALLS 15

    Offerings: Adam & Eve
    Refusals: Cain & Abel
    The Sacrifice of Isaac
    Magnificat
    No Warning in Bethlehem
    The Judas Tree
    Grand Piano
    Thomson's Horizon
    Family & Rainstorm, 1955
    The Parables of William Kurelek
    The Horsemen

PART THREE   FROM *SO THE MOON WOULD NOT BE SWALLOWED*   29

 A Honan Dustsorm
 Good Housekeeping
 A Chinese Evangelist
 Evacuation
 Lunar Eclipse
 She Writes of Her Garden

PART FOUR   WHEN THE HOUSE IS FILLED WITH SPACE   37

 Canticle
 Sonnet
 Balcony Haiku
 Easter Ghazal
 Villanelle
 Let Beauty Come
 Routines & Recurrences
 Silence Raves

PART FIVE   OUT OF REACH   49

 What Will Be
 Hints of the Hidden
 Seeing Is Believing?
 The Lake
 Even as All Creation Groans
 Droplets
 The Vandal of Vanity
 Shadow of a Truth
 Like Your Voice on a Long-Distance Call
 Other
 Sixteen Functions of the Moon
 Feet-First
 Creed in a Minor Key
 Cycling
 Auschwitz
 The Heart of a Grocery Cart Is a Wayward Thing
 Hands

As a Baker
Wind
The Weight of Glory
The Talbot River

PART SIX   MEDITATIONS   73

Meditation #1
Meditation #2
Meditation #3
Meditation #4
Meditation #5
Meditation #6

PART SEVEN   POIEMA   81

Poiema

Acknowledgments

I WOULD LIKE TO thank Luci Shaw, John Terpstra, Richard Osler and Bruce Soderholm for their generous assistance in editing these poems for publication.

Many of the poems in this collection—although perhaps altered here—first appeared in the following publications: *The Antigonish Review, Arc, Canadian Literature, The Christian Century, Christianity & Literature, Christian Week, The Cresset, Crux, The Dalhousie Review, The Fiddlehead, First Things, Grail, Mars Hill Review, The Nashwaak Review, Perspectives, Prairie Messenger, Propaganda, Quarry, Queen's Quarterly, Radix, Rock & Sling, Stonework, Studio* (Australia), *3.1.6, Wascana Review, Windhover,* and *Windsor Review*; thank you to their editors. "Routines & Recurrences" first appeared in *The Wisdom of Old Souls* (Hidden Brook Press, 2008).

The poetry in section III is a sample from my chapbook, *So The Moon Would Not Be Swallowed* (Rubicon Press, 2007); thanks again to Jenna Butler for her faith in me. "She Writes of Her Garden" has since appeared at LiturgicalCredo.com and "Lunar Eclipse" was reprinted in *The Fellowship Link*.

I would also like to thank the following for their encouragement: Hannah Main-van der Kamp, Jill Peláez Baumgaertner, Denyse O'Leary, Hugh Cook, David Kent, Doug Koop, John and Marion Franklin (Imago), my sister Ruth Maude (Dandelion Web Design), Ken Fox, Ross Muir, Joan Eichner, my friends of The Word Guild, and my friends in the delightful writers group that meets in our home. Thanks to those who have hosted readings, and to everyone who's purchased my chapbook. Love and appreciation to Gloria, Nathan and Caleb for enduring my eccentricities and preoccupations. Finally I would like to thank Diane, Ted, Tina, and everyone else at Wipf & Stock for making this happen.

Soli Deo Gloria,
DSM

Part One

Worlds Descend from Worlds

Cædmon

a poem for the first poet of English

There are certain times you're as comfortable
as the babe settling down in the sweet hay of the manger
& others   when you see the harp being passed   hand
to hand   getting closer to you   song
by song   & as the music continues to swell
the hands that are sure upon the hay fork   become
wet & tingly   so you wipe them on your breeches
& swallow a little of the monks' warm ale
but it doesn't steady you   or do anything for your swollen
languid tongue   & still the harp moves closer
so you slip out to the stable to be sure everything's
right with the horses   though why wouldn't it be   seeing
you've already rubbed them down   & picked their hooves
clean   although fresh clumps steam in the stalls
as a large shape shivers in the darkness
recognizing the way you move   As his tail swishes   & hooves
clomp on the clay floor   you reassure the beast
& tell yourself   as you settle in the straw
you'll return to the glaring lamplit clamour of the feast
as soon as you find your breathing
But that's when the angel appears   lifting
you from a sleep you've fallen into   like from a dark well
& he calls you to sing
You stammer a protest as Moses did
but he calls you to sing
a song of the creation of all things
& *that*   is the beginning

Behind My Eyes

The feeling behind my eyes is older than my eyes
its roots run deep   deeper than the hollowness
of what wouldn't come early in school
deeper than the birdlike way attention settled on a branch
then left it swaying   abandoned

Did it begin behind my father's eyes
reflecting London Ontario in depression
when his mother died
& his father was left standing
a barren maple on a winter street?

Did it begin behind my mother's eyes
in a boarding school in China
where her parents' love came by mail
(when the mail could get through)
a blossom dropping petals in the rain?

I've ripped out every trace of that feeling
like the cedar shrubs from our back garden
whose roots I battle each spring
but I know   oh too well
what's just beneath the surface

Part One   Worlds Descend from Worlds

These Things Never Change

The boy lives in the now   unchanging patterns of lying down & rising up
within the sound of his mother's voice
where the hands of the clock return to the same place every morning
Hear the boom of his tennis ball (slap shot from the point) against
the garage door   Hear the vibration of bicycle tires on the street
These things never change

He once believed the truth of his father's fictions   about once being a boy
not always a father   & that there once was a world without *him*
but no more   Nothing changes   not really
The now is everything   there's no progression
He's always been able to ride   no hands
& he knows violin lessons won't lead to music   not really

The now is everything   & yet it bounces astray
becoming something strange
& unpredictable like a ricochet off the goal post
The boy lives in that disorienting now that crept out of yesterday's
But that's just how it's always been
These things never change

Living in the Shadow

Once I admit the element
of drama   Once I admit
poetic licence   Once
I admit various perspectives
& canonical questions
things aren't as simple

This love floats mid-air
where history unpredictably whirls

When my great-great-great-grandfather came here
    before Toronto was Toronto
When my great-grandfather from the other side
    arrived about sixty years later
After another sixty plus years
    as the city lay before me
but then it was not the same place

Cities descend from cities
Worlds descend from worlds

Family trees
filled with testifying birds
seem immutable from root to tip
but branches
thicken with new growth
like new poems rewrite old

I live in the shadow
of ancestral faith

Ipperwash Beach could not be constant
over sixty summers   over four generations
since no strand's the same the following day
Promises are difficult on a windswept shore

Part One   Worlds Descend from Worlds

Worlds keep turning   Waves keep breaking
We are sandbars long submerged

But my faltering doesn't disrupt
the galaxy's music

Once I admit my faith is small
love alone secures my inheritance

Censorship

She is so far away that his words take more than a month
to span the gap   Based on this equation I am more than
800 times further away   down a one-way street
holding his words in their guarded   plastic sleeves

He must be careful what he says   Even an orderly
in the ambulance corps needs to be censored
so he speaks in generalities   of their destination
& their activities   & of her brother with trench fever

The moon moving through the clouds
sings of his loneliness   & of the girl on Princess Avenue
down whose sidewalk his mind freely moves
even though an ocean & a war block his way

He censors himself   for the blind ping pong of their
relationship is like the image of a horse-drawn ambulance
moving beyond a line of trees   though perhaps
as unnerving & unpredictable as "Fritzy's big guns"

Her most recent response is to something distant
& preliminary   She doesn't know
that after eighteen months he's finally advanced
through dangerous terrain to the word   *love*

A quarter of my genetic makeup is in the hand
that pens the words   & a quarter in the hand
that eagerly opens the envelope   & so I know
in my bones what he can only hope

Part One   Worlds Descend from Worlds

The First Five Days—Amiens

On day one of the big offensive
more than half of those he tended
in the dressing station   were prisoners
In the operating theatre he'd seen
soldiers having   bullets removed
shrapnel removed   legs

On day two   her month-old letter
came right up to the line   & found him
busy with the wounded

On day three   they marched
taking shelter in a barnyard   while biplanes
battled overhead   one—two—three   German flyers
brought down in flames within fifteen minutes
That night he slept   peacefully   beneath an apple tree
right through the shelling   until the morning barrage

On day four of the big offensive
he didn't know where the line was
or even their flanks
just that they'd come eighteen kilometres
from where the push had started
Returning   he found the unburied bodies of horses
& Germans   He started a letter to her
on some captured paper
That night the countryside lit up
when bombs hit an ammunition dump
Spooked horses bolted in wide-eyed panic
pulling his   & other ambulances   on a wild ride

On day five   he discovered the bombed-out roof
of the dressing station where he'd read her letter
making their prisoners
carry the wounded   bury the dead
In every field he passed   there were small mounds
marked with crosses

POIEMA

Tribal Burial Customs

"During life serve your parents, when dead bury them, afterwards sacrifice to them, thus you will be filial."
—Confucius

Some in coffins underground
some in small houses above ground
some wrapped in cloth
some cremated
some tied tree-top with roots & vines

Some held for mass interment
with twenty years of corpses
Some buried face-down
for fear the spirit will find its way
back to haunt the living

Some just after death
heads wrenched violently around backwards
so spirits will see the living
are making appropriate arrangements
Some just before death   Some before death

Some delay burial
until they can afford
the mourners' fees & the geomancer
who knows of earth & air currents
& of the hostile paths of evil spirits

Some a year later
re-open graves to wash frightful bones
for seven trembling anniversaries
or longer   if the clan's troubled by tragedy
before finally leaving them alone

From the late Walter Tapscott Steven's biography of his father, Arthur: a missionary to tribal China & Burma between 1883 & 1903, & my great-grandfather.

Part One   Worlds Descend from Worlds

Ode to an Antique Sideboard

after Blake

An oak of distant time   must have swayed
its fearful mass   dark leaves   in dreadful whispering
of high winds in the forest of the night
What sinews must have twisted & whirled
from deep root   to skies
before a hand & shoulder
before an axe & chain   dared bring it low

But that was long ago
before it was hauled to the dark planing mills
before the craftsman seized it
& framed its symmetry
before the grain whirling in the tree
whirled in the oak face of the furniture
that the craftsman smiled to see

In another time   it must have taken its material place
in the heart of one whose eye aspired
to the art of home decor   her mortal hand
gracefully arranging china tea cups
symmetrically within the frame
of the bevelled mirror
which reflected the hearth fire burning bright

Did he who made the tree's grain whirl
smile at the craftsman's creativity
the pleasure the first owner had in its integrity
or your joy at making it our own?
An oak of distant time   must have swayed
its fearful mass   dark leaves   in dreadful whispering
of high winds in the forest of the night

Adrift

At every desk   in every row
a head bowed low   to scribble
as chalk dust on them settled
Unable to focus on the teacher's talk
my thoughts soon drifted away

His lilting words lost meaning
making listening of little use
like the sum of the square of the hypotenuse
adrift with Henry Hudson
abandoned on Hudson Bay

Without a sail   a small boat
grows smaller in the distance
aimlessly afloat   without provision
like a boy lost to procrastination
without hope for a better day

Time is a coin   to have but not to hold
a silver moon sailing a cloudy sky
I was always too young
too young   & then too old
as that moon sailed away

Part One   Worlds Descend from Worlds

The Pump at the End of the Lane

I remember the sound of the pump at the end of our cottage lane
the bray of a donkey   the song of an old man who knows only two notes
We would pump & pump until rewarded with the gush
we knew would come   because it always did   four kids
taking turns   cupping hands   while another worked the lever
our throats filled with icy pleasure
We splashed each other   & ran from getting soaked
clothes clinging to limbs   flattening hair
but drying quickly in warm summer air
& then we'd pump some more   the sound
rising with the level in each pail   to the edge and over the brim
sometimes soaking into the soil   sometimes puddling on the ground
but always obedient to its watery way
& then we'd return to the cottage   carrying our sloshing loads
handles hurting hands   precious liquid spilling over the rim
Oh   to be like water   in praise of him

Mongrel Mind

To see me now you'd never know   how in my early days   my stray mongrel mind would wander without warning down dark alleyways   My eyes would have given it away   their sky suddenly filling with cloud   then glazing over like a time-lapse film of ice forming on the surface of a pond   Something as simple as a math calculation would be interrupted by an unexpected door swinging open at an inopportune time   Without ever even moving   my escape was rapid   rabid canine cunning carrying me mentally across barren tundra   beneath desert skies   with no thought of what would have been best   It was like a series of unseen obsessions strong within the nasal passages   to be sniffed out along the fenceline   followed & followed   & howled of when inaccessible on the other side   & then forgotten as soon as instinct sings its next song   It was like being distracted from a book's singular plot by its unlimited possibilities   like reading a ripped map with the treasure X torn away   like running in the dark across a field of stubble only to stumble in a rut when expecting it least   At any time   logical progress could be stopped cold by a trunk filled with trinkets   In another dimension   a trash can could clang when tripped over & my attention would be gone   bounding down empty streets   even though seemingly engaged within the confines of a narrow room   Perhaps it was a strange weakness in the hinges of the imagination where doors   sealed of necessity   would widely yawn like guards carelessly asleep on the job   Perhaps it was also a strange strength   a wilful wildness   like a thundering buffalo herd as opposed to the usual pack mule   Perhaps only unleashed minds catch the scent of abstract concepts   erratically riding the King's highway   In the alchemy of my thinking   like the ironic law of the kingdom   I've learned to turn a flaw into the essential rule

Part Two

The Knife Still Falls

Offerings: Adam & Eve

Adam had always said exactly what he thought
honest to a fault   like an apple that would ripen
ripen   & eventually rot   not
knowing when to stop   not
considering how Eve might feel
when he'd chosen to not
take another walk with her through the garden
leaving her to encounter the serpent alone

He'd never
had to work through his childhood   never
had to deal with difficult relatives or in-laws   never
had anyone choose to not
take another walk with him
Eve had always been more subtle   more astute
smiling tactfully at the half-wilted
uneven bouquet he'd offered to her
each flower ceremoniously named
There's rosemary & there is pansies
there's fennel for you & columbines   he'd say
She would simply smile & offer him fruit

Refusals: Cain & Abel

Cain had always been proud of his produce
the second finest garden   to date
in the history of humankind
but his understanding was often slow
to ripen about certain things
such as the way his brother had sliced
a lamb like a soft melon   spilling juice
on the ground   for Cain had sacrificed
from the fruit of the vine
Abel had always said that that was like offering
the wool without the sheep
but Cain could only think of wool as like the rind
& refused to think his gift was second rate

Out in the field the argument grew deep

Cain's hoe thudded into a plump pumpkin
chopped fiercely into the hills of potatoes
& split their thin skin
As he refused to be his brother's keeper
it spilled & spattered the tears of tomatoes
before they drained into that soil deeper & deeper

Part Two   The Knife Still Falls

The Sacrifice of Isaac

God told Abraham   *Kill your son for me*   & they
climbed Mount Moriah so there would be a great
distance of rock   cloud   shadow & light to be sliced in
two   & the perplexing covenant might come to mind as
you stare toward the blue horizon

The knife seems to fall forever
as Abraham (looking like an old man Rembrandt
frequently sketched) palms the bound youth's face
with a large determined hand to shield him from the
sight

The knife seems to fall forever
giving you time to think of bloody Passover   of Jesus
as sacrificial lamb   of what kind of god would ask so
much   & what kind of father could do it (as a
windblown angel seizes the old man's wrist)

Then you notice the eyes   bloodshot & observant
of a ram caught in a thicket   This is no happy ending
Three centuries after Rembrandt
the knife still falls

Magnificat

Our starting place must be
with the breath of God moving through
two women   like a forest fire through
a stand of dry cedars   crackling
with the prevailing desire of the wind

The flames flare in their flowering wombs
where their unborn sons stir
before touching these mothers' tongues
so that mysteriously conceived words
flicker into the air

But there's more to this communication
than a woman's lips parting
in response to her cousin's *Blessed are you*
How did this navigate its way
into Luke's account?

Our conclusion rests
with the fiery breath   our belief either
in words   faithfully remembered & passed
from tongue to ear   or reignited
by the same spark in the doctor's heart

Part Two   The Knife Still Falls

No Warning in Bethlehem

She never knew of the decree   her husband had slept
through the night   & there'd been no angel warning him
in a dream   before death came marching into Bethlehem

The banging on the door was no warning   it burst open
splintering along the hinges   The three   four rough soldiers
the crying of her boy   & then her wail alone filling the air

The arms of her husband   his faithful words   useless
She was as far beyond consolation   as ashes beneath a grate
are beyond returning in their original form to the forest

Her agony   her questions would only shift slightly
if she learned of the foreign star-gazers who'd made a boy
the target   or of the angelic intervention in his escape

She had no warning that her son   would die in place
of his son   no hint this wrong would fill with right
in the fullness of time

POIEMA

The Judas Tree

Cercis Siliquastrum

From within the alabaster skull of a man
better off unborn
throbs the pressure of regret
The hand that dipped into the bags
        that dipped bread in the dish
        that reached for bloody stars
now scatters to the ground a silver constellation
for the burial of aliens
& strangers

Too late   No return   Too late
The garden's salty kiss of blood
stains his lips   ripe
as Zechariah's prophesy
Irretrievable
as the spikenard of devotion
He grasps for consolation in the word   *friend*

Bloody blossoms hang
from the cursed Judas Tree

Part Two   The Knife Still Falls

Grand Piano

The grand piano is unintrusive
sharing the livingroom
with Glenn Gould's chair
& with alphabetically filed acorns & pine cones
waiting to sprout amid armchairs
into perfectly memorized forests

Startled pheasants jump-start our hearts
Delicate notes like their feathers
descend form the ceiling   from the trees
yet accumulate nowhere
Each variation like a butterfly on film
rewinds into its cocoon

Greatness has lost its greatness
We walk right through the wide-mouthed instrument
yawning
without bending strings or bruising shins

Thomson's Horizon

We don't believe in silently falling forests
despite convincing theories   or the soundlessness
of oil on canvas   See how Thomson's horizon
is so low   as if seen by one in a heavy-laden canoe
dipping his paddle   closed in by hills & trees
Is there any other way to see the world?

As we walk toward *Northern River*
the path is springy beneath our boots   or rock solid
nothing less than it appears   & so we trust our senses
to keep us from tripping over fallen branches
or over other visitors to the National Gallery

We rely on the miracle of our receptivity
to the natural realm without really considering
its significance   We agree the dabbings of colour
mean autumn underbrush   the dark lines mean trees
but what do the underbrush & trees mean?

We study his obsessive studies of sky & clouds
more concerned with   seeing what the artist saw
as he dipped his paddle   considering what he considered
to be a suitable subject   as he swirled his brush
Are we ever able to express what we see in the world
without saying more about ourselves?

Part Two   The Knife Still Falls

Family & Rainstorm, 1955

As Alex Colville has painted it
a young mother watches an approaching storm
across the wide river

She holds open the door
of their mastodon sedan
for her children to take shelter

The interior of the door is as plain
as the fifties   The solid lines
of automotive bulk point to the darkening sky

The pleats of her white dress are real
The yellow grass beneath their bare feet
is real   so is the coming rain

I wasn't even born then   but as I watch
the family entering the car
I know   the rain is almost upon me

POIEMA

The Parables of William Kurelek

I

On the geometric prairies
there is only earth & sky

The sower   fires up his Massey-Harris
to scrape the landscape
like a painter with his canvas

On seedbags   & the fenceline
that pulls your eye to the emptiness of distance
sit the fowl of the air

They follow the tractor
devour the seed where it falls

II

The house & barn & silo are bathed in moonlight
Their shadows are filled with stillness

From the height of the painter's imagination
we see into the sleeping bedroom

The gate is open   & Satan's horses pull
deceit through ecclesiastical fields

III

The family has gathered like sheaves
on the front lawn for a photograph
The gathered generations
like the distant trees of the Ontario countryside
speak of Autumn   not noticing
the dogs gathered at the foot of the cross
the mushroom cloud over Hamilton

Part Two   The Knife Still Falls

The Horsemen

Inspired by the woodcuts of Albrecht Dürer (1471–1528)

In the depth of a dark dark night   down in the ravine
the wind comes up & stirs the leaves of the myrtle trees
where a corral of shadowy horses grow restless
Your approach is barred by a rider on a red horse   his hand
rests on the hilt of his sheathed sword   You ask   *Whose
are these and why are they here?*   His reply   *Come and see*

But that's when a thundering voice shouts   *Come*
& a powerful white stallion pulses from the black woods
Its rider has an arrow notched in his bow   The wreaths blow
back from his hair   & from the garlands in his horse's mane
We are the ones sent to roam the earth   the first rider says
to ride to the four compass points & to hold back the wind

Beware the coming of pestilence   he continues   *Beware
the coming of wild beasts that leave a country childless
the coming of famine   & the one*   he adds as his heel
digs into his horse's flank   *the one who brings a sword*
He too rides off as the voice roars   *Come*   leaving you
alone beneath the breathing myrtles

You walk toward the whinnying herd   & see starlight
shimmering on their coats   brown & black & white
red & dappled   *Come*   the voice echoes through the ravine
& a black horse & rider race past   almost hitting you
with the scales he carries   He shouts   *No bread
no bread   but plenty of distractions for the well fed*

You feel drawn to pick up a three-tined pitchfork   & toss hay
into the corral   The strong horses push against each other
begin to kick & bite   You offer hay to a skeletal   pale nag
He doesn't fight   as you impulsively climb onto his back
You lift the trident in your hand   With unexpected strength
he surges to a gallop at the sound of the command   *Come*

Part Three

From So the Moon Would Not Be Swallowed

A Honan Duststorm
(January 1924)

Wind & dust & the barrow-man squinting
with dirt in the creases of his face
unwilling to take the young husband   & U Shu-mei
to another windswept village

Dust & wind & the east gate closed
too far   through swirling dust
to another dusty gate
several li away
They decide not to go & are grateful
when dust settles   & they hear
that that village is full of bandits

Wind & dust & dust & wind
The young wife   prays in Yencheng
The young husband   watches from some outstation
The wind blows where it will

Good Housekeeping

Finally   war is over
trains are running
mail's coming through

"I cried for joy over your precious letters"
so many letters & the latest
Good Housekeeping (March 1926)

Her "most pressing need" now is help with Marie
Spend more time with your child   her reading says
Take her for walks away from the usual surroundings

But there's so much teaching to do
& walks are taboo   The beach is horrible
with blood & memory of war

The beheaded & shot were buried in sand
but dogs will be dogs
in China as elsewhere

Part Three   From So the Moon Would Not Be Swallowed

A Chinese Evangelist
(October 1926)

They love darkness because their deeds are evil
I love it because I slipped away
The room dark   like the shadow of a sheltering wing
They lined us up
I took a deep breath   hit the floor
& rolled under a bed
lying for two nights beneath the robber-chief's breathing
more his prisoner than when he had me
He inhaled   I inhaled   He exhaled   I exhaled
sleeping & not sleeping
the nightmare of their game   again & again

    They line up ten men
    How much land do you own
    The first says   three acres
    & they shoot him
    The second man lies   eight acres
    & they shoot him
    The third says   fifteen
    They shoot him when they find he lied

My fellow evangelist died   in truth   this way
When I redream it I am in the line
or they drag me from beneath the bed

Each waking I try not to move
my limbs silently scream   surrender
but there's purpose in my escape
they hiss   strangle out the breathing
but I pray for deliverance
some other way

When moving out   the breathing's voice says
check under the beds
but they miss one   & I escape

Evacuation
(Early 1927)

From deep in a box car
the open countryside south of Yencheng lies
Rice fields & peaceful hills
flow like the Yangtze

The children sleep amongst baggage
to the soothing rhythm of rails
oblivious to danger behind
or danger ahead   enemy territory

If you unload twenty five pieces
of luggage quickly
as the train pulls out
the trail might be just fifty yards long

Innocent dreams of railyards rise
like black puffs from locomotives
undisturbed by the changes of trains
& territory & soldiers' uniforms

Undisturbed by filthy berths   broken engines
& three days & nights in the belly of insecurity
Dreams as seamless as if all trains are one
all days are one   & all tracks lead to Hankow

Part Three   From So the Moon Would Not Be Swallowed

Lunar Eclipse
(June 1928)

Yencheng, Honan, China

On Sunday evening as darkness crept in
the people rushed out
with gongs
    & pots
        & anything to make noise
to scare the heavenly dog
that slowly
    very slowly
        ever so slowly
had placed its jaws about the moon

They persisted in their din   it was said
so the moon would not be swallowed
& leave them in the dark   forever

She Writes of Her Garden
(June 1930)

My Grandmother writes of her garden
wallflowers & cornflowers
from early April showers
like beautiful wounds healing across the bed
from blue to purple to dark pink
to light pink to white
& then geraniums in May
But she cannot see the geraniums

She writes of her garden
from the cool of the cellar
where she cannot see zinnias explode
with life or blood-red roses
contrasting the portulacas' flesh
An armoured vehicle is sowing shells
(not cockle shells) broken glass
between the rows of flowers

She writes of her garden
not so much of the British Consul
asking missionaries
south of the Yellow River
to evacuate to Hankow
but of yellow marigolds
& hollyhocks
& Japanese sunflowers for the house

Part Four

When the House Is Filled with Space

Canticle

> "... *music puts our being as men and women in touch*
> *with that which transcends the sayable, which outstrips the analysable.*"
> —George Steiner, *Real Presences*

Explain the flight of the Great Blue Heron
not in terms of aerodynamics
but in relation to morning fog   to rippling lake
Imagine a dove descending & a voice from heaven
proof only to those who need none

Think how a string quartet says so much
like waves on the Lake Manitou shore
matching the music of rooftop rain
in our waking minds   like David's harp
soothing Saul's madness

There's a myth that sings of a song so beautiful
sailors forget themselves
forget to eat   forget they're vulnerable
on rocks   Unimaginable
to those who've not felt it

Sing your jealousy to a nightingale
of her oblivion of weariness
fading into night
Sing your longing to a waterfowl
of her wise way on the pathless coast

Follow the flight of ravens to Kerith
where Elijah drinks from the brook
until it sinks in sand
like a half-remembered melody
fading in time

POIEMA

Sonnet

after Jane Kenyon & Psalm 96

Let every planet follow its orbit
Let the prevailing winds blow where they please
across the water   May the moon move seas
in tides   high on the Bay of Fundy   It
is not within our strength to make it quit
Let every lake reflect all that it sees
so paths of light will shimmer   May the trees
reach skyward   & every flower submit
to its own blooming   May all on the earth
cycle down paths that follow their calling
like migratory birds' instinctive ways
Let rain & snow give in to their falling
& babies in the womb to their own birth
But mostly   may this all be done as praise

Part Four   When the House Is Filled with Space

Balcony Haiku

1. Holy Ground

> A horizon tree
> blazes in the setting sun
> but is not consumed

2. City Lights

> No stars in the sky
> tonight they all are scattered
> on the ground below

Easter Ghazal

Bound by winter's fist when the air is chilly
a buried bulb's the dead memory of a lily

The empty shell of a loved one   in a closed coffin
lies still   as we all will   beneath a lid draped with lilies

The green shoots surprise us   no matter how often
we witness soil first opening to a hint of lily

Its green rapidly rises   then cone buds soften
white trumpets opening   disguised as lilies

Each   silent as the stone that sealed the tomb   until he
blasts on that trumpet   then we'll rise like a lily

Part Four   When the House Is Filled with Space

Villanelle

I call out to you Lord   answer my prayer
I search your map   but you stay out of sight
Why do I sometimes feel like you're not there?

I follow your wind down long highways   dare
to presume   that you'll lead me to some height
I call out to you Lord   answer my prayer

Instead I crash   convinced you really care
despite glass shards   bent metal   & doubt's bite
Why do I sometimes feel like you're not there?

I drive my wrecked dreams in for your repair
you dismantle them   & close for the night
I call out to you Lord   answer my prayer

I sit in the waiting room   unaware
if you're ignoring me   or if not quite
why do I sometimes feel like you're not there?

What good is it for me to always stare
into the darkness   waiting for your light?
I call out to you Lord   answer my prayer
Why do I sometimes feel like you're not there?

Poiema

Let Beauty Come

Psalm 90:17

Let beauty rest on us   like a shaft of light
penetrating to the dimness of our forest floor
our eager green turns toward it

Let beauty come   like rain for Hopkins' roots
splattering exuberantly on our disappointments
making right what we could never foresee

Awaken our hibernating senses   so we find
what was hiding   & what was on its way
The affirmation of blessing

Let beauty grow in the work of our hands
not our own   but truest beauty
growing in the work of our hands

Part Four   When the House Is Filled with Space

Routines & Recurrences

(a pantoum)

At ninety-six she's seen here all she'll see
She's learned to laugh at her own confusion
Her days fill with routines & recurrences
It's as though her memory has become full

She's learned to laugh at her own confusion
She can't remember taking her walk today
It's as though her memory has become full
She can't keep track since each day's much the same

She can't remember taking her walk today
Names & dates of those who love her slip away
She can't keep track since each day's much the same
Someone she doesn't recognize speaks her name

Names & dates of those who love her slip away
Her days fill with routines & recurrences
Someone she doesn't recognize speaks her name
At ninety-six she's seen here all she'll see

Silence Raves

In his darkest night the man of silence raves
So much is given & taken away
Hanging like a dried leaf in the February wind
blown against a mindscape of all he's read
& all he's heard   Words   not from his thinking
not from his feeling   not from him at all
echo through his skull
brush the sensitive quadrants of his brain
spoken again & again

In the man of silence his darkest night raves
My beseeched embrace I freely give
So much is given & taken away
His eyes shut darkness from his hearing
I'm fearing for his wholeness
through his irrationality of the heart
I listen to the flow of adrenalin
hold tightly to his words
spoken again & again

In the night of man his darkest silence raves
Words suppressed for a lifetime
spoken again & again
an incantation to turn the world aright
He raves on (too loud too loud)
in the hearing of the whole house
his children   his grandchildren
(the youngest not ten days old)
So much is given & taken away

In man the night of his darkest silence raves
My impatience suppressed at his elegy
spoken again & again
What of after the funeral   when family's gone
when the house is filled with space

Part Four   When the House Is Filled with Space

when the traces of her tastes & encumbrances
linger like a fragrance?
So much is given & taken away
Blessed be the name of the Lord

Part Five

Out of Reach

What Will Be

We sense it in the call of a Canada goose in flight   a longing strong enough to carry an entire flock to their destination
   We feel it in the grumble of a distant storm   that dark dissatisfaction at what is   in comparison with what will be
   The people who should never let us down   let us down   The cabin roof groans with the weight of so much snow   The stairs in the old farmhouse complain with every footstep   even with the memory of feet that move no longer   The branches of an enormous oak moan in the high wind
   We hear it in the spirituals nurtured in the cotton fields of the deep south   a deep hopeless sorrow distilled into hope for beyond   *Comin' for to carry me home*
   We may think we merely imagine it in the whistle of a train as it rumbles through a midnight crossing   but the tracks through BC's mountains were laid with the blood of Chinese navvies   the sweat of abandoned dreams   & the boxcars rolling through the prairies during the depression   carried the last hope of the unemployed   Don't imagine that that wail   has nothing to do with human grief
   Sometimes our wounds heal completely   sometimes they leave a scar   A woman learns of cancer in her breast   a man finds his heart is failing   We fall to our knees for a miracle   & are startled when an answer seems to come   a taste of what will be   Hear the wind in the cavity where the siding is loose   Hear it banging against the wall   Sometimes our wounds don't heal at all
   We fall to our knees   but the sky grows grey   featureless & silent   We long for what we had   what we almost had   what will be
   We sense it in the stillness of a beaver pond   or in the rush over Niagara
   We see it in the sunflower   pushing through the soil reaching for the sky   for the sun   When we most identify with this world   we are most unsettled

Hints of the Hidden

Warm sun reinforces our denial
Summer's faded
like the slip of the birches' vivid green
along the colour wheel to an immaculate yellow
Such   seems incompatible
with decline & fall

We slip on gloves to cycle the valley
the rise & descent of small hills
shifting gears of delight
The hillside is alive with death
coagulating on the branch tips of maple
& sumac   pooling on the ground

Every familiar guise of our world   reflected
in the smooth creek face   hints
despite utility's slippery deception
of the hidden
in the way beauty tumbles into beauty
the way meaning detains our attention

Part Five   Out of Reach

Seeing Is Believing?

If seeing is believing   how do we see beyond
mountain ranges of cloud   in mountainless landscapes
beyond sailing ships sinking below the horizon
into the depths? Our language shimmies
awkwardly ignoring our knowledge
of receding glaciers & rising suns

We believe what we do not at first understand
The meaning of crimson creeping across
the extent of a leaf   the depth of turquoise
in a mountain lake   Seeing is believing
they say   although we know
colour happens within our perception

Were John's senses sufficient to comprehend
what he saw   when he saw the One who was
& is   & is to come   surrounded
by seven lampstands   holding a fistful of stars?
Was his vision a poem within living experience
granting a depth we wouldn't otherwise know?

Believing is seeing   such as when the outline
of the house you know is there materializes
from the snowstorm's depths to save your life
An act of prayer will contribute to healing
they say   giving substance to things hoped for
though unseen as through frosted glass

The Lake

The lake's skin is so thin   it's a wonder
you can cross at all   To sit in a kayak
is to sit in the palm of her hand   your craft
convincing her to hold you as one of her own
cradled in the hollow of each gentle wave
The lake is a mother   is a daughter
whose mood shows in her transparent face
As boldly as on solid land   you venture onto the water
weighing the solitude   presuming upon her grace
where   really   you have no rights

The lake is a martyr   is a physician
your paddle piercing her miraculous skin
As soon as you extricate its blade
she will heal herself   the swirling circular scar
will fade   spreading out to nothingness
her colourless blood dripping back
to her heart   from your paddle tip
When you're alone with her   listen
for her kiss on the hull of your kayak
There's nothing she will not share

The lake is a lover   is a prophetess
testifying of the sky   Beware
when her face grows black   & she invites
her wind to toss you like a fallen leaf   Beware
her hindering headwind
halting all progress   Beware
her capsizing crosswind
slapping your ambition down to despair
proving once again
here   really   you have no rights

Part Five   Out of Reach

Even as All Creation Groans

Deer Lake (23 February MMVIII)

    Beneath the frozen February stars
the silence echoes off distant shores
& the shackled lake mutters
of its escape   with a baritone thrumming
a grumbled gurgling caught in its icy throat
    A pillar of smoke rises
from the abandoned campfire
built right on the ice
an insult to the waters beneath
a reminder of their chains   like Orion's belt
drawn tightly across the midnight sky
    The rhythmic scrunch of my boots
describes the crisp cold snow
but once they come to a stand still
the quiet complaints of the waters rise
like bubbles from the muddy bottom
or the mournful memory
of a century of bullfrogs' moans
from the summery marshes along the shore

Droplets

Across the crowded classroom   along
the wall of windows   the raindrops
clinging to the glass   conspicuously catch the light

Beyond   everything appears darker
the green of trees   the dampness of pavement   the
dull-edged shadows across the ground

No sound comes through the double pane
I walk to the window   observe light rain's random patterns
on the puddles   the slick sheen across the blacktop

Once more I'm caught by the trickle of a droplet
flowing & merging into another   pausing
reluctant to lose its singularity

Just as the scene outside is inverted within my eye
& then flipped again within my brain
it is turned on its head   within each drop of rain

The top-side bulges with the dark blur of evergreen
& red brick from townhouses across the street
the bottom   with the brightness of the featureless sky

I find the kingdom of heaven in a droplet
the thirsty are satisfied   & the king kneels
to wash his followers' feet

Part Five   Out of Reach

The Vandal of Vanity

Don't think of me as the night walker
the shadow stalker   the vandal of vanity
smashing your tasteless treasures
Think of me like Gideon of old
trashing Baal's altar
& chopping down your Ashterah pole
I do a service to the neighbourhood
plucking each plastic tulip
& kicking over the kitsch
of wooden woodpeckers with whirligig wings
Think of me as a politically incorrect public servant
doing what you wish you had the nerve to do
The cliché of pink flamingos has been
outlandishly outdone   by pine cut-outs
of fat ladies' backsides   bent over their gardens

My city needs me   to decapitate
all offending garden gnomes
to smash your ceramic frogs
(if your car's left unlocked
I'll even grab your bobble-headed dogs)
& pulverize your plaster elephant planters
Under cover of night   I'll set things right
decommissioning the ice cream truck
with its irritating tinny song
destringing lop-sided strings of icicle lights
that would hang there   all summer long
Somehow you think we can't see them
because you've not turned them on
In the morning   when you waken
they'll be gone

Shadow of a Truth

A child holds a truth in his hands
smooth   solid & full of reassurances
He watches the way it catches the light
& glistens upon the far wall as he turns it
Its unnoticed shadow is dark & ominous
on the hardwood floor   all one & indistinguishable
from the shadow of his own hands

He goes for a long walk
that leads back to where he started
There's a change   sudden & violent
or as gradual as the appearance of grey in his father's beard
He trips over his own feet   (part of growing up)
trips over a truth that refuses to throw spears of light
breaks it down into pieces that don't easily fit back together

He sits in his parents' livingroom   examining
what's in his hands   disappointed by how coarse and dull it is
His eyes look past to the floor   focus on what's cast there
He might let his playfulness manipulate the shadow
find its beauty as he did in the glistening   years before
He might decide
shadow is all he's ever known

Part Five   Out of Reach

Like Your Voice on a Long-Distance Call

Like when the stuffing slips from a cushion
that's grown threadbare
my grandmother's soul   found a frayed edge
that permitted passage   orientation shifting
from one life to another

Like a radio tuned to a different frequency
or a dog's floppy ear twitching
with sounds beyond our range
as her mouth fell open   her eyes brightened
comprehending something we didn't

Like a pathway in her mind for her soul
to return upon   my grandfather opened the hymnal
of their lives   pouring tea & snatches of song
for her tongue to trace back   as steam rose
& disappeared somewhere near the ceiling

Like your voice on a long-distance call
or a child crying out in a dream
my grandmother's soul went
walking some distant shore   past   present
or   what was then   yet to come

Other

From an upstairs window
he views his neighbours' house
From their upstairs window
he views his own house
This is not quite what I want to say

He walks past a mirror
trying to see his profile
trying to see what he looks like
when he's not wondering what he looks like
This is also not what I want to say

From early childhood truth gradually eroded
his position at the centre of the universe
Once when they were picking teams
he shared the look of the unselected
of not wanting to be last

He daydreamed what it would be like
to identify with some alternate reflection
to see someone else as himself
to see himself as someone else
& to not be given a second thought

In an upstairs window
he views his strange reflection
older than he remembers
not knowing who   or how
not knowing what he wants to say

Part Five   Out of Reach

Sixteen Functions of the Moon

I

To pull the oceans like a bulging eye
meditating the Bay of Fundy into an expanding lung

II

A sister to the sun
& a lesser light to rule the night

III

To nudge the waters of equilibrium
flowing toward the ear canal
inching a madman over the brink of Niagara
like Ophelia asking too much of water

IV

To contrast all with virtue under the moon
symbolizing inconstancy with her borrowed sheen
her horns toward the west or horns toward the east

V

To predict the weather of the heart
as the sea gives up its dead
beneath the moon's corona

VI

A dreamland of green cheese & dry seas
from where the man-in-the-moon
can wink at our ambition

VII

As written in the Book of Jashar
to stand still in the sky over Aijalon
while hail stones the Amorites

Poiema

VIII

To mark months on the walls of imprisonment

IX

For freezing a tom fence-top
blood dancing cold & wild
mesmerized by the phases of the reflector
reflected in kindred eyes

X

To hunt the clouds as the Lady of Wild Things
the lover of Endymion glistening on the hillside

XI

For the exile of Cain
and the gatherer of Sabbath kindling
with thorns upon his back

XII

A field for the gathering of stones
a driving range for heroes of the sky

XIII

To make fools of lovers   of poets
& of those consulting the moon in high places

XIV

To be blown into an eclipse of the sun
a process in the tearing of the curtain

XV

To interrupt the eye's inward focus
(a crescent hooking through the retina)
snatching it up to the sky

XVI

To be turned to blood & darkness
as old men dream their dreams

Part Five   Out of Reach

Feet-First

Being born breech
may be cause or indicative
of my hesitance to head
head-first into anything

My first tentative leap
from a dam on the Trent Canal
plunged me feet-first
into a parallel submarine world

In my shrinking youthful searches
I cautiously tried the waters
unaware how quickly they drain
out of reach

Oh there's no need to tell me
faith is tough
I've tested it thoroughly
inch by inch

POIEMA

Creed in a Minor Key

I believe in the subtle realities of the universe
that reveal themselves to those who have eyes
to see   ears to hear

Witness wave patterns of wind through the wheat
of the visible & the invisible interweaving
across the surface of the water

Consider the birds of the air   that never consult
a map or check a calendar   Number the stars
& calculate the distance to where it all ends

Witness the bare branches that reach skyward
all winter   crossed sticks against a blank sky
awaiting the fullness of time

Consider the lilies of the field   that never concern
themselves with trivialities such as death
but wither   with certain spring in their bones

Witness how a little light can dispel darkness
the way the moon testifies to a glory not her own
that no bushel can contain

Consider the storyteller's instinctive template
of conflict & resolution   Contemplate the root
& offspring of Jonah's three days in the belly

I believe in the ram caught in the thicket   the bread
that came down from heaven   the bronze serpent
suspended   & the dry path through the Red Sea

Part Five   Out of Reach

Cycling

Twenty four wire spokes   evenly spaced
carefully tightened   so the weight shifts smoothly
like lines of longitude spinning us through
another amazing day

Commonplace magic   is still magic
even when feet push pedals as thoughtlessly
as they step   (the arch curving as on a ladder's rung)
every movement as precise as fingers on keys
automatically playing a minuet

Within the mystery of physicality
the way the body accepts mechanical limbs
& the mind absorbs experience
a cyclist is a new creation
an earth-tethered bird   a waterless swimmer
making all things new

The kingdom of heaven is like a cyclist
rolling through an imbalanced world
No matter how common our perception
every spring   (our tilted axis coming around)
another child straddles the wonder
without training-wheels

Auschwitz

When our video ended we flicked on the news
The fiftieth anniversary of the liberation of Auschwitz
A survivor claiming to be an atheist said God
took a seven-year vacation
I thought it strange to criticize a god he doesn't believe in
but I don't have to live with the horrors he's seen

    Our children sleep as snowflakes
    accumulate in our silent yard

We'd just been watching *Tender Mercies*
Robert Duvall is a country singer
with enough hope to climb from a bottle
After his daughter died in a crash
he's hoeing the garden
as if to break up the big questions

    Our children sleep as snowflakes
    accumulate in our silent yard

I know two men whose wives are dying
Blurry prayers are all I have to offer

Part Five   Out of Reach

The Heart of a Grocery Cart
Is a Wayward Thing

Shopping carts flow like rain   down & down
to the lowest point in the parking lot   congregating
like sweltering cattle   beneath the shade of a field's only tree
Always park at the point of highest elevation   at the A&P
or one may gore your car   when they instinctively dart
in a chrome lightning flash   a stampeding
grocery cart cloudburst   (to inextricably intertwine
the metaphors)   escaping from surprised seniors
who hadn't expected such heart

It has no wish to be caught   You've seen what happens
once a buggy roams beyond the confines of the supermarket lot
Do they climb to the top of the highest lookout
watching the skies   like a prophet of the end times?
Do they repent & roll their way back to the grocery store?
The heart of a grocery cart is a wayward thing
seeking a ditch to wallow in
Shopping carts flow like rain   down & down
into any convenient creek

It is here they fall into bad company   becoming bent
& broken   often losing a wheel   rusting & falling apart
Is there no redemption for the prodigal shopping cart?
Might they not be washed clean   washed downstream
into the nearest of the Great Lakes   wheeling down
the St Lawrence & out to sea?   How great it would be
if they evaporated like ocean spray   & were carried
to the clouds   where they might once more fall
down & down   upon parking lots   as rain

Hands

for Gloria

Like chubby dimpled paws   like diminutive
versions of inflated kitchen gloves
they try to grasp some purpose
enclose a parent's outstretched finger
Ah   this is solid   this has meaning

We build with hands   church & steeple
hide ourselves   then peek through
like ten moons rising over valleys of skin
We open doors   place a finger on it
learn what counts   or at least what to count on

Emerging identity silently circles each digit
leaving its invisible mark   We close fists
get out of hand   but reaching fingertips
find the joy of fingertips   hold on open-palmed
Ah   this is solid   this has meaning

So here we are   fingers
intertwined like vines that hold fast
held by the freedom of being held
Volition secures from within   deeper
than skin   than blood vessels   than bones

Part Five   Out of Reach

As a Baker

    As a baker she's a maker in a holy tradition   the daughter
of a farm daughter from Manitoulin   bringing delicacies to my mouth
    Her fingertips understand the transformation of flour   to
dough   to flaky pastry   & how to stir my attention
    She makes music with raspberry & blueberry   with strawberry
rhubarb & cherry   takes the humble apple   spy   cortland   mutsu &
macintosh   & mystically   with perfectly unmeasured cinnamon
bakes wonders
    She wakes my senses   makes sweet squares at Christmas
brings forth fruit pies   cobblers & crisps   in season   or draws
delicacies from the deep freeze   a large serving of summer   cooled a
long age in winter's deep well
    She shakes my appetites alive   with tastes & textures on my
tongue   For my sake she'll shake & roll & sprinkle sweetness in her
kitchen alchemy   She knows the way to a man's stomach   is through
his heart   making me receptive to all she has to bring   tuning my palate
to her particular talents   developing my dependency on her presence
her smile   her voice

Wind

for G. K. Chesterton (& for Caleb)

The child in my arms
watches wind
stir leaves & draperies
He's learning what is real

He's no language
for breeze   or breath   or spirit
This nebulous trembling
hasn't crept as close as other familiar movements
a wagging pendulum   or the tumble
of his mother's hair towards him

We learn   wind is just wind   through naming wind
We speak of wind   as our parents
& their parents   spoke of wind
Although this wild & startling world
won't explain itself   the dust returns
to its consistent settling after every storm

Although there's more than he'll know
the child in my arms
watches   & wants to understand
He's learning to be at home here

Part Five   Out of Reach

The Weight of Glory

Stand at the foot of an enormous oak
follow its bulk upward
where decades swirl   unseen
within the clenched fist
of significant fibre
see how it all unites   climbing
with perpendicular purpose
to where it spreads across the sky

At the height of day
the thickest limbs   the thinnest leaves
protect us   in their small way
from the full weight of the sun
Balancing in their branches
it bleaches every detail away
washing out the extended hand
into a formless silhouette
telling us nothing about the sun
about leaves   about branches   about the hand
except light   light   light   light   light

Slip out from under the oak's domain
as heat yields to cool evening
as light   to darkness
Stare into the endless face
from where innumerable suns shine
upon forests & grasslands
Look up   this new splendor weighs
on your weightlessness   whispering
The world is charged with the grandeur
& the weight of his glory

POIEMA

The Talbot River
(97/98/99)

for Nathan

You can't cast twice into the same river
although it looks the same as in the photo
of that first fishless summer
where the shimmering rays surround you
like an icon of boyhood   as you bend into your reeling

In the darkness we come down to the beach
to those renewed waters   (where you have caught fish)
We   in our joy   are the fish-like swimmers
where the hook-shaped moon dangles from heaven
& I still long for what is out of reach

Part Six
Meditations

Meditation #1

Like the wide-winged eagle brooding on her aerie
the unlimited power that made the world
submitted   (oh   curious thought)
to the limitations of humanity

Lower than angels   confined by time & space
The bread of life   after forty days   felt hunger
The living water   dehydrated on the cross   felt thirst
& became obedient to death
(so death   pride-wounded   would die)

Like the eagle turning & turning in widening arcs
he ascended   to be the right hand of power
yet submitted   (oh   curious thought)
to the limitations of humanity in us
as he builds his limitless kingdom

Meditation #2

Yahweh walked the garden in the cool of the day
giving Eden's children a chance to hide
Through the intervening years   he spoke aloud
or wove images through whispering dreams
until finally   he stepped into our skin

These are the echo days   every divine sound
reverberates from the past
so we listen to the silence
amid the distractions of the world we see

Longing for faith by sight
we squint into the half light   half blind
complaining as weeds try to choke us
yet the cares of this world hold less danger
than meeting holiness face to face

Part Six   Meditations

Meditation #3

That first bite surprised her   the fruit was so delicious
The serpent smiled down   as if to say   I told you so
She now knew the pleasure   first-hand
& luxuriated in it before learning the sting of its after-taste
She'd known so little   yet crossed the indelible line
taking the rest of us with her   If she hadn't known any better
she wouldn't have known any worse   but she did

When we lift our eyes to the hills
the grandeur gathers   though it wears man's smudge
When we look to the stars   glory's declared
though we often turn away   Taste a good tree's fruit
in season   See the moon shimmering on a northern lake
What is it inside us that interprets the world accurately enough
to implicate us too?

Meditation #4

A man was going down from Jerusalem to Jericho
when he fell among thieves   & the God of heaven
watched as they beat him   stripped him of his clothes
& left him for dead

Oh   if only the Lord had sent the priest
to distract them from their intent
If only the Levite had come earlier
but their robes swished by above the surface of the dust
caught in an ecclesiastical conundrum

Then a Samaritan came
(& my heart sings God's praise at this part of the story)
but what of the one who falls
where even God seems to pass by
on a road where no Samaritans travel?

Part Six   Meditations

Meditation #5

Our entire livingroom safely fits within a camera
carried through the latest war zone
(or within the wake of famine   earthquake
or tornado)   & even from the fridge
machine gun fire's still audible

What do we do to each other?
Why won't God intervene   or does he
when true emotion flows from our stony hearts?
Our sin   hardly explains the fall
of buildings that have been crumbling for years

But when we reach out (for a moment)
to our neighbours on distant roads
God might (for a moment) be glorified
in our eyes   the eyes of a generation born blind

Meditation #6

The olive trees deepened from their particular green
to grey   & then to black   The master walked through the grove
trailed by eleven of his bewildered band
Take this cup from me   they might have heard him say
had they not fallen asleep   Their distractedness troubled him
Sleep on   he finally told them   (This I understand)

But right from when the priest's official struck his face
through each cutting word   cutting whip   & piercing nail
so often   instead of forgiving
I'd have called for the legion of angels

Instead he hung there like the bronze serpent
in the wilderness   & shouted   *My God   My God   Why*?
(This cry I understand)   Until he gave up the ghost
as the noonday skies deepened to grey   & then to black

Part Seven

Poiema

Poiema

A man steps   motionless
from the shallow depths   the unwinding labyrinth
of his childhood
                a piece of work
crafted by innumerable chisels

Have you ever stood   somewhere
where the wind & waves have worn the rock
magnificently?

He walks along the cliff & looks blindly
out to sea   with a focussed inattention
that had been modelled so well for him
& yet   little things loom large

The lines of a poem have no knowledge
of their beauty & precision
they're formed from the same stuff
as backyard banter & letters to the editor
They find a glistening where least expected
like midnight stars at the bottom of a well
They speak of what's been overlooked
& trodden under   like miniature morning glories
speckling a lawn

He finds a gnarled old cedar   in tableau of a dance
it does on the storm-beaten coast
limbs in graceful submission to the missing wind
its trunk gradually curved in response
to the downward slip of its foothold
roots grip the rock & help hold
this little bit of the planet together

Along the dunes a woman walks
far from the roaring silence of her past

Poiema

Her every day is a learning   a turning
from what she thought she knew   & from
what she didn't even know she thought
& yet   the Holy Spirit smiles through her
& her kindnesses

A tree is planted by a seed on the wind
or by a squirrel   or by a kid with a good arm
from the back seat of a Buick
Even more so   we are His workmanship   His poem
& yet are oblivious to so much

www.ingramcontent.com/pod-product-compliance
Lightning Source LLC
Chambersburg PA
CBHW072010090426
42734CB00033B/2415